SUPERPENDEJO

By
James Wallestein

I dedicate this book to the immigrants
who leave behind their countries, start a new life
and work very hard to have a better future.

INTRODUCTION

Hello reader.

The first thing I want to tell you, is that everything I narrate in this book is 100% true.

This story will blow your mind. I guarantee you have never heard anything like it.

This is the narration of the bizarre life of a man so incredible, so amazing, so crazy and so dynamic; that it is very difficult to believe that it really happened.

Precisely for that reason, because it is such an extraordinary story, I think it is very important to share his story and let people know nothing is impossible.

In addition to being fascinating and very entertaining, it is a story that has many lessons and morals that can be of help to many people.

The protagonist is real. I worked with him for almost six years: I was his boss.

I know the story first hand; we were good friends and coworkers.

Other people from his life, such as other coworkers, his neighbors and friends; they also explained many things to me.

From what I saw with my own eyes and from everything he told me during all those years; this man has truly lived a daring life.

When making this book I had doubts about how to tell the story.

Among all the different options to choose from; in the end I chose to move away from novelizations, fictions, dramatizations, etc. and tell the story without additives, exaggerations or modifications: a chronological narration of events, moments and conversations in the first person, from my point of view, as I lived them.

The disadvantage of this narrative format is that it does not follow the conventional structuring of stories in three acts: introduction, development and outcome.

But the advantage is that the story is more pure and real, with a documentary style, very direct and without frills.

At the end of this book I will give my personal opinion of this man, the protagonist of this book.

I say to you truthfully that this is not a racist or discriminatory story. It is simply a true story and it happened just as I'm telling it. Some parts you will like and some parts you will not, but all the parts are true.

I have changed some names and details to preserve the anonymity of both the protagonist and some people who worked with him.

Thank you very much and enjoy this exciting story.

James Wallestein

"Pendejo" is a profanity Spanish word that is very popular in México.

Mean: a stupid or contemptible person.

So "Superpendejo" is a very, very, very stupid person.

CHAPTER 1

1952 Nicaragua - Central America.

In northwest Nicaragua there is a municipality called Esteli, near the Honduras border.

There is a small rural farming village, in the middle of the jungle and mountains, called Pueblo Nuevo.

There the protagonist of this story was born: Antonio Toledo.

When I met him in 2012 he was a 60-year-old man: gray hair and mustache, and he was 5ft 2inch tall. He was not muscular and had a noticeable belly. He did not drink alcohol but he liked to eat.

His most notable physical attribute was his smile: he was a good, honest person, with a good heart but above all very happy; a very positive person.

His father worked in the fields; he was a farmer and he was illiterate: he could not read or write.

Antonio Toledo walked the dirt, unpaved streets of the town, playing along with other children.

But when he grew up, he soon began to work in the fields helping his father and learned agriculture.

Antonio went to the small school in town, and he held the books with his hard and calloused hands, the hard hands of a peasant, but he did not finish learning to read: when he was nine years old, he dropped out of school.

Antonio Toledo worked very hard, all day everyday; all he did was work.

He had no ambitions, no dreams.

He did not like to drink or smoke. He never tried drugs.

He didn't like expensive things either: he was a conformist. He could wear the same pants and shirt an entire decade until they broke.

And so he grew into an adolescent, and then into a young adult.

On page 5 of this book I have described what Antonio Toledo was like when he was 60 years old. Imagining him at 16 is not difficult: his same face without wrinkles, his hair and mustache black and thin, and of course without a fat belly.

He earned a reputation for being tireless: he worked hard in the fields, twelve and fifteen-hour days, always with a smile.

I can attest in the years he worked with me he was a tireless, positive, serious and excellent worker.

Then he met a very humble girl of his age, from the town, and they started having sex at the age of sixteen.

Antonio loved sex: he needed it daily and sometimes several times in the same day. At that age, that passion is understandable.

At the age of seventeen he married his first girlfriend and moved into a very humble little house, almost a shanty made from old pieces of wood.

Shortly thereafter his wife became pregnant and gave birth to a baby.

Antonio was a father at seventeen years of age.

He worked very hard in the field and when he got home all he thought about was fucking. He desperately needed to fuck.

His wife had her second child at eighteen:

And then the third

And then the fourth

And then the fifth

And then the sixth ...

He had a total of 19 children in 20 years.

This is 100% real; Antonio Toledo and his wife had 19 children.

I would laugh talking with him about his sexual relations with his wife and I would say: ¨Antonio, damn... You always had your wife pregnant. She gave birth and it didn't take long for her to get pregnant again and again, for two decades. That was inhumane for that woman. She was a baby factory machine! ¨

Antonio just laughed like a kid.

I joked with him saying: "You didn't have a television in your house, did you?" He was laughing like a naughty boy.

It is a fairly popular joke in Spain that you say to people who have many children.

When you're at home, television is supposed to entertain you, relax you, and finally put you to sleep. But if you don't have a television, you don't know what to do, you're nervous and don't feel like sleeping: that's when you see your wife and think about ... You understand me.

Without television there is a much greater chance that there will be sex at home. And when you have many children it is because you never had a television.

Of the 19 children that Antonio Toledo has had, the truth is that his wife had a set of twins but both died at seven months of gestation. It was a very difficult abortion.

Two other children died as well, one around three years old and the other at eleven.

A fifth child died years later, at the age of five in 1987.

Altogether Antonio Toledo had 14 sons and daughters who lived but the death of his fifth child, in 1987, opened his eyes.

Antonio Toledo always works very hard, tirelessly and with his eternal and contagious smile, but they continued to live in a leaky shack.

His children had dirty and old clothes. They played with sticks and empty food cans. They had no toys.

They were poor people in a peasant village. What he earned was not enough to give a dignified life to all those boys and girls: to give them good clothes, food and care.

His son, who died in 1987 at the age of five, died precisely because they did not have money for good medical coverage. He became naturally ill, developed a condition, had no medical care, and died; like a stray dog without attention.

It was then that Antonio Toledo decided to do something to adequately provide for his large family: earn much more money. Thus his children and his wife could live with dignity.

But in that humble little town in Nicaragua that was an impossible dream.

Until someone told him that he could emigrate to the United States of America, where he could earn mountains of money.

And that became his ambition and objective: to emigrate to the United States.

But how could he achieve that if he was not a qualified professional, had no career and was practically illiterate?

Then a natural disaster happened but for him it was a blessing.

In 1991 a volcano exploded in Central America.

It killed several thousand people in various countries but most of all it destroyed roads, infrastructure and worst of all it destroyed the crops of various countries.

If those countries were already poor, with the loss of the crops, this could turn into a humanitarian catastrophe.

Then the United States of America granted work visas to the people affected by the volcano.

People from Nicaragua, El Salvador, Honduras and other countries could migrate to the USA, work and send money (dollars, currency) back to their families and thus help support the economy and reconstruction of their origin countries affected by the volcano.

This part was never fully explained to me, but presumably someone helped him do all the paperwork, presented it, and he was approved and got a legal visa to live and work in the United States.

Thus in 1992 Antonio Toledo went to the United States: without knowing how to read, without knowing how to write and without knowing a single word in English

CHAPTER 2

1992

Dallas - Texas - United States

Antonio Toledo emigrated to the United States when he was 40 years old; but he was not alone.

Several companions from the town and Nicaraguans from all the country went together and supported each other.

They rented a three bedroom apartment.

-He slept in one bedroom.
-In another bedroom, in two beds, stayed a father and his son.
-In the last bedroom slept another companion from his home town.
-On the sofa in the living room slept another Nicaraguan.

In total, 5 men lived in the apartment and divided the rent for the apartment.

Rent was $700 a month in 1992, they each paid $140 a month.

As I have explained, Antonio Toledo had no hobbies or ambitions.

-he never went to restaurants
-he never went to the cinema or the theater
-he had no television in his room
-wore his same old faded clothes for decades
-he never went to a sporting event
-he never stepped into a McDonalds

Antonio Toledo explained to me that this was the only way to save: not to spend money on anything.

All he had was a small radio in his room; where he listened to Hispanic stations and the only food he ate was Maruchan noodles, which Hispanics know as "Maruchas."

Antonio Toledo only drank tap water, no sodas, no juices: absolutely nothing. All he ate, when he rested on his days off, in the apartment were Maruchas.

This was what his days off were like: talking to his Nicaraguan roommates, listening to the radio in his room, drinking tap water and eating maruchas.

Antonio Toledo's monthly expenses were about $200 between the apartment and food.

Antonio Toledo worked in a hotel, and after his expenses, he sent ALL of his money to his wife in Nicaragua: about $1,400.

And that was his life in Dallas: working, sleeping and when he rested listening to the radio, eating maruchas, drinking tap water and living like a beggar.

No ... there are beggars in Dallas who live better than him. They eat at McDonalds, watch TV, and drink Coke!

CHAPTER 3

1992

Nicaragua

Here it is necessary to speak obligatorily (so that the reader of the book understands the context) of how one lives in Nicaragua, the cost of living and what things are worth there.

The average monthly salary in Nicaragua in 1992 was about $80.

If the man and the woman worked in a family, a middle-class family would earn a total of $160.

In the capital, urban and modern area, a 3-bedroom apartment was around $300.

In a mountain town, with dirt roads, without sewers or asphalt in many areas, the price of an apartment would be $150.

Therefore, the money that Antonio Toledo sent to Nicaragua each month was equivalent to 18 WAGES.

That is a lot of money for Nicaragua.

A mountain of money.

Antonio Toledo lived as a hermit but had achieved his dream: to generate a lot of money for his family.

So in that little Nicaraguan town they bought a little plot, they built a wall around it and they built a two-story house with eight rooms inside.

A huge house.

By the average standards of the village it was like the Kardashian mansion.

In which there lived his wife and his 14 sons and daughters.

They bought a refrigerator and it was always full: lots of meat, vegetables, and sodas.

Antonio Toledo ate Maruchas, but at least he had the consolation that his family in Nicaragua ate very well.

They even had new clothes! Sneakers!

And when the big moment came they bought a great TV for the living room!

Antonio Toledo listened to the radio, but at least his family watched color television in Nicaragua.

CHAPTER 4

2002

Dallas - Texas - United States

Antonio Toledo was in that dynamic for about 10 years.

Living like a hermit and sending all his money to
Nicaragua: after a decade around $ 170,000.

The man always worked very hard and had no expensive
ambitions or tastes: he was humble and simple.

But he loved one thing: fucking.

His 19 children hadn't magically emerged, had they?

Then he met a humble but very hot Mexican woman.
Outside of work she was an alcoholic, but she loved to fuck
at all times as it was.

And Antonio Toledo did that: fornicated with her like a rabbit, day and night.

Many times she slept in her own bed at night.

She had her own place to sleep but she was a nymphomaniac.

Antonio Toledo told me all of this verbatim.

He did not like that she was a drunk, but oh well, the man had to put up with somethings he didn't like in exchange for having all the sex he wanted.

Antonio Toledo was so thrifty that in those 10 years he had never returned to Nicaragua to see his wife or sons and daughters.

They only talked on the phone.

Ten years without being in contact with his family.

Antonio Toledo said to me: "Why am I going there? Plane flying is very expensive. Also when you are there you are not working and you do not make money. Also when you are on vacation you don't stop spending money, lots of money with so many children around."

Brutal.

I said to him: "Antonio man: not everything in life is working and saving. There are times when people take vacations, spend money and have a good time. You have a family. You have to be with them and see your children grow up. They need to see you once a year for a couple of weeks."

But he was stubborn.

"Antonio. You have a wife. She is still young. She needs your contact, your hugs, kisses and love."

"She has had a lot of contact with me every night for twenty years: she has given birth to a bunch of motherfuckers." He answered me.

The point is that after living 10 years in the United States and working very hard, Antonio returned to Nicaragua for the first time.

CHAPTER 5

2002

Nicaragua

Antonio Toledo took a plane and landed in the capital of the country: nobody was waiting for him at the airport terminal.

He took a taxi and a few buses until finally; after several hours, he arrived in his hometown, where he was born, where he grew up, where he married and had children.

The white painted house was impressive. It was big, very big.

His sons and daughters received him very coldly — there was no joy or smiles. His wife acted the same. No one grabbed his bags to carry into the house.

"Where do I leave the suitcases? Where is our double room?" He asked.

His wife asked him to follow her.

They crossed the ground floor of the house, came out to the walled backyard where it was full of plants sowing and where there was a large kennel for two dogs that were circling there.

Next to it was a small shed where they kept the tools to cultivate the patio. She had thrown an old, stained mattress on the floor, with no sheet or blanket on it. "That is your bedroom, in there." Said his wife.

"But what are you talking about?" Antonio was no longer smiling. He was confused and didn't understand anything.

"In Dallas you were fucking every day with that Mexican whore. Cheating on me. You and I are done: I want a divorce." She said.

At that point in time Antonio learned several interesting things.

Antonio Toledo discovered, but never knew, that one of his roommates, was a gossip and had talked with Antonio's wife by phone and informed her of her husband's activities in Dallas.

In my opinion whoever did that is a son of a bitch.

Another interesting detail is that when the wife learned of his cheating, she said nothing.

She wanted to continue receiving those huge amounts of dollars every month from the United States.

The point is that Antonio Toledo was almost illiterate.

And his wife had put all the money in a bank account only in her name. The land and the house were in her name.

Antonio Toledo after ten years working very hard and living like a monk; in reality he had absolutely nothing.

His oldest sons who where obviously angry, looked at their father very seriously and asked him to leave the house.

After being humiliated with the shed and the old mattress, he was kicked out of the house.

Antonio Toledo, in shock went to a motel, he spent only two weeks there feeling very sad. He did not go to visit other family members or friends. He was not sexually involved with any village women.

He returned to the airport and returned to the United States.

As he told me: "I do not like to fight or argue. Let her keep everything. I'll find myself another woman."

At 52 years old, Antonio Toledo started again.

CHAPTER 6

2002
Dallas - Texas - United States

Antonio Toledo returned to the hotel and continued to live in the same apartment with the other Nicaraguans.

He never bothered to find out who had gotten away with his wife's gossip. He did not care.

Then an era of sexual liberation began for him. He could fuck with want without explaining to anyone.

After returning from Nicaragua, the Mexican drunk wanted sex with him, but he did not want to because she was an alcoholic and did not give him a good feeling: he wanted another type of woman. She said okay.

When he wanted to realize, since she visited him a lot in his apartment and slept many nights with him, he knew all the men who lived there and fucked them all. At four.

She came at night, everyone drank and everyone took turns going to one of the rooms to fuck her one after the other. Several times. As she was a nymphomaniac having sex half a dozen times every night and with several different men it was great.

One day Antonio Toledo walked in the neighborhood in the afternoon, one day he rested.

There was a blonde woman, with long straight hair and slender. He started talking to her and she was from Guatemala.

She was very nice and Antonio took a strong risk: "Do you want to come to my apartment to fuck me?"

She smiled and answered yes.

They walked hand in hand down the street until they reached the apartment.

They hugged and kissed in Antonio's room. She gave him a delicious blow job. Then he wanted to fuck her.

She said, "No problem but first I want you to know in case you haven't realized yet that I'm a crossdresser, a man."

Here are various versions of what happened next.

Antonio told me that he told her to please leave her apartment, and he never saw her again.

Antonio also told numerous times that he was so hot that he fucked her.

What is the true one? God only knows.

On another occasion a coworker named Garcia told him that there were some blue pills that put the dick like a steel bar.

He offered to give her one but keep in mind that:

A) He had a girlfriend to relax the steel bar with sex.
B) You only ate half a 100mg pill because they were very powerful.

Total that when Antonio Toledo gave him the pill he laughed so much thinking that everything was a tease and a lie that he swallowed it whole in front of García.

On the one hand, since he did not have a girlfriend, he could never use the pill properly.

On the other, he had an erection so violent that it lasted four days.

There are doctors who say that if after eating a Viagra you have an erection of more than two hours, you should go urgently to a hospital to relax your penis with medication. Because the blood being so long in the penis can form clots.

Antonio Toledo broke all records with his four-day erection. Surely the blood in his ears coagulated too.

He walked for work with a tent in his crotch.

Everyone laughed or stared in shock at his pants, the very obvious boner.

Then one day he received a text message from a resident lady of his hometown.

She was single and they started texting.

She said to him: "I need a responsible man who knows how to take care of a woman and I like him: he seems serious."

And they started a distance relationship, online.

CHAPTER 7

2012

Dallas - Texas - United States

I went to work at the company where Antonio Toledo was: he was his direct boss.

And I learned about everything that has been told in this book so far: both by Antonio Toledo himself and by other colleagues.

Yes something characterized Antonio Toledo and his smile is that he always had in detail everything that was happening to him.

He was not shy or reserved in that regard. It had everything in great detail.

At that time, he had already had a virtual relationship with a Nicaraguan woman for ten years.

It was incredible because many times I saw him talking to her on the phone, saying many nice things to her.

In those years, from 2002 to 2012 he had sent her about $ 200,000.

But something happened: his sons and daughters contacted him, the same ones who kicked him out of their own home.

Now they were all kind and good sons and daughters. They asked him for help to come to the United States illegally.

Antonio Toledo would pay all the expenses of moving one of them, so that he travels from Nicaragua to northern Mexico. There, he would pay a coyote (Mexicans who know the border region and act as guides to illegally move an immigrant from Mexico to the United States) about $ 3,000 to pass his son or daughter.

In total with all expenses and the trip about $ 5,000 to $ 6,000.

A son passed by and when he arrived he disappeared and never contacted his father again.

The same thing happened with her next child and so on.

They were very kind and very good children on the phone, they begged and pleaded for help to their father, and when they crossed the border they disappeared.

Not all of his sons and daughters went to the United States: only 11.

The other 3 had their lives organized in Nicaragua and did not want or need to come to the United States.

Of his 11 children who illegally immigrated to the United States, 4 were deported: drunk, after car accidents ...

So they called their father again.

Antonio Toledo replied: "I have helped each one of you once and it has cost me a lot of money. If living in the United States you have screwed up everything is your fault and problem. Don't count on me again. To have used the head."

Those 4 children never called their father again.

Of those 11 immigrant sons and daughters there was one exception, one daughter.

A daughter that her father did not pay anything: her boyfriend who lived in the United States did.

She and he were boyfriends in town, he went to the United States and now she was helping her to come.

She came and disappeared in a Bus Station.

When Antonio Toledo telephoned her this was more or less the conversion:

"Where are you my daughter?"

"I'm in Michigan."

"What are you doing there? Your boyfriend is very concerned. "

"I'm living with another man, the one I really love."

"And who is it?"

"Another man from the village."

WOW.

In other words, the woman had that TWO boyfriends in town at the same time: one who loved and another who did not.

And he took advantage of the cost of the trip and the coyote to the United States to go with him who he really loved.

Why didn't that man pay the trip and the coyote?

Because they grabbed the other boyfriend and like a subnormal paid for everything: they took advantage of him.

I talked a lot about this topic with Antonio Toledo.

I told him that except for his daughter and those who stayed in Nicaragua, 10 of his daughters' sons had used it to come to the United States.

That they really didn't want him as a father.

Antonio Toledo answered me:

"I don't care if they love me or not: they are my children. I have helped what I have been able to each of them as it is my duty as a father. If afterwards they didn't want to know anything about me, I don't care."

Antonio Toledo spent between $ 50,000 and $ 60,000 bringing 10 of his children to the United States and they never thanked him.

CHAPTER 8

2013

Dallas - Texas - United States

Antonio Toledo was already 63 years old.

And he always works very hard, more than five boys of twenty together. Something impressive and admirable its vitality.

Always with that eternal smile, his great sympathy and that contagious natural joy that made everyone around him happy.

She had been with this new Nicaraguan for ten years and had never seen her in person! But I had sent him about $ 200,000.

At that time the strategy as a couple was different, and thinking about the future.

They bought a large piece of land in the Nicaraguan town, built a one-story house with several rooms, and began buying animals: several cows, a bull stallion, and a donkey.

The idea is to make a kind of small farm with rabbits and chickens, milk from cows, sell foals, sell the older ones to butchers, etc...

In my ignorance as a city person, I asked Antonio Toledo: "What do you want the donkey for? What is his role on the farm? "

And he told me it was to ride the donkey and walk his farm and land with him, because he did not know how to ride a horse.

Okay. It makes sense: walking your properties on horseback, but you don't know and you don't have a horse, because you ride a donkey!

So with a lot of bought animals and the small farm finally working after ten years Antonio Toledo returned to Nicaragua again.

CHAPTER 9

2013

Nicaragua

Antonio Toledo flew by plane and arrived in the capital of Nicaragua: this time no one was waiting for him at the airport either.

After several hours, with taxis and buses, he arrived at his farm.

Counted by him.

He hugged that woman, younger than him, around thirty-five years old, and she was living at home with her cousin, who went to live with her on the farm because he helped her a lot.

Her cousin was a tall, athletic man of thirty, younger than her.

He was very nice and kind.

And there was Antonio Toledo fucking desperately day and night.

The woman never said no to him, from day one.

And after two weeks of vacation, Antonio Toledo, very satisfied with his wife, the farm, his animals, etc... returned to the United States.

When he arrived two things happened.

One night he called her and her cousin answered. Said, "She is sleeping."

And it didn't take five seconds for her to reply. Were they sleeping together in the same bed?

In Mexico there is an expression: "Sancho".

A Sancho is the lover of a woman: the one who warms the bed of the husband who is never at home.

And I said to him: "Antonio… That supposed cousin showed you his identity document? You really don't know if he really is her cousin or not. It could be her Sancho, her lover, who lives with her on the farm and also works on the farm with her."

Antonio did not like that kind of comment.

He show a photo of once they went to the beach and it was incredible.

Someone took the photo. Antonio Toledo standing, in shorts, smiling, and in the background sitting on a towel his wife, the cousin next to her very close, putting his right arm around her.

WOW.

There was a lot of chemistry and partner complicity in that photo.

I said to him and his co-workers: "That cousin is his Sancho."

And he refused to admit it.

One day she called him and said it was all over.

That like the house, the farm, the land, the bank account and all the money that was in it, EVERYTHING, was his because he kept everything.

That happened with him in Dallas, United States, and she in Nicaragua.

And so that love story ended.

I asked Antonio Toledo about it: "Everything has stayed. What are you going to do? Find a lawyer. Go to Nicaragua and fix that problem? What are you going to do?"

And he replied: "I don't care. Let him keep everything. I have lifted a weight off me and I no longer want her. I want a younger woman, worth her while. "

And so he did.

He never claimed a penny of all that money or property.

He literally worked eleven years very hard, drinking tap water, eating Maruchas, always wearing the same old shirt, never gave himself a whim, never went to a McDonalds, lived as a hermit to give everything to that woman and help ten children who they never thanked him.

CHAPTER 10

2014
Dallas - Texas - United States

When I asked Antonio Toledo what his ideal as a woman was, he answered me very simply.

That She fuck a lot and that is 20 years old.

In 2014, Antonio Toledo, 62, was not exactly a beauty.

He was fat, gray hair and mustache, and he didn't have a tooth: he had dentures. On top of that, he had developed Psoriasis on his elbows (some colleagues, who had seen him change his clothes one day at work, said that it was also on his knees).

His elbows were like the back of a mangy dog. No creams or medicines were given.

Garcia, his coworker, joked with him.

He said that he once had a mangy dog, that all his hair had
fallen out of his back and that he had brutal psoriasis and
that he bathed it with used car engine oil and that he
cured himself and it was shiny on top of it.

García volunteered and told Antonio Toledo to go to his
house, that he had a barrel full of used motor oil behind
him, to put on a swimsuit and go inside for a while.

That would cure her psoriasis and leave her skin glowing
like new.

Obviously Antonio Toledo never accepted the offer.

Antonio Toledo had another much bigger problem: he had
cataracts in both eyes.

The fleshiness were so evident that looking at his eyes
closely you saw them: it was something horrible.

You gave him a piece of paper and wrote:

HOUSTON
CAR
LEMON
BREAD

And he read smiling:

POTATOE
BEE
HAND
HELICOPTER

He made up words because he was unable to distinguish letters and he was half illiterate.

I said to him: "Antonio ... In 22 years you have sent $ 170,000 to two women who have kept that money. You haven't enjoyed any of that money. Save money, and in a year you take two months off. You go to Nicaragua with an appointment already made, you have two eyes surgery the day after arriving there and you stay in a hotel for two months resting and recovering, with some girl from there taking care of you. A cheap plan and nothing difficult. Without eyes or vision it is very difficult to live and work. Fix your eyes. "

He never listened to me.

His mentality is that it was a very large expenditure of money.

Just like going to a McDonalds was like going to the casino, because operating your eyes was a lot of money spent without sense.

Very sad his way of thinking. He never put his health ahead of or prioritized it.

55

Sometimes in the morning, while sleeping, I would call my phone and answer it thinking it was an emergency. It was Antonio who was so blind and did not distinguish the contacts and numbers on his phone that he was confused, and instead of calling his girlfriend he called me by mistake.

Every time he did, he laughed like a child.

Today in 2020 he still does not have eye surgery.

You have to make a mental image of Antonio Toledo naked.

Imagine a 35-year-old woman in bed naked and standing opposite is a small, 62-year-old man with a beer belly, psoriasis on his elbows and knees, toothless, with gray hair and mustache and blind as a mole. It is not an image that excites many women.

The woman for almost $ 200,000 that she received, having a free farm and house, etc...

She and her Sancho decided to swallow with that man in Nicaragua, whatever it was for the money.

But the taste of that drink was so disgusting for two weeks, she suffering and her Sancho rabid inside, that after Antonio left they said: "For this shit we don't go again. We already have money, the house and the farm. There's no need to swallow that old man again. "

And so she ended up with Antonio Toledo.

I think if she knew how gross it was to sleep with him numerous times she probably would have broken up with him before her trip to Nicaragua.

Or perhaps they were afraid of how he would react to a breakdown.

But when they met him in person they realized he was a harmless asshole.

That there would be no problem if she ended the relationship.

Antonio would never ride his donkey again.

CHAPTER 11

57

2014

Dallas - Texas - United States

Then a woman texted to her phone number.

And Antonio Toledo started another online relationship.

This time with a Nicaraguan black, full face, with large breasts, in her twenties.

And Antonio Toledo sent him ALL the money, as he had done with the other two previous women.

She was from the same Nicaraguan town.

And so it was two years.

CHAPTER 12

2016
Dallas - Texas - United States

Antonio Toledo was 64 years old.

And he told me that he was going to break up with that girl.

"Why?" Asked.

And he told me a terrible story. Apparently she was always sick, continuously. Hospitals, medicines, trips to doctors, medical bills even under the carpet, etc...

Later, she had a six-year-old boy who called him dad and kept asking him for money for clothes, books for school, etc...

Antonio Toledo had bought so many books for school for this boy that he could open a library in that town.

Damn... The kid read more that fucking Albert Einstein.

The girl's mother said that if she wanted to talk to her, she must pay for it.
Antonio Toledo said to me: "I don't like my mother-in-law. Every time I want to talk to her I have to send her money through Western Union."

"For talking to her?" Asked.

"Yes." He answered me. "Her daughter doesn't ask me for money for talking to her but she is always sick. I am not liking it because she is a very weak and sickly woman. "

Two years sending money to a woman that you have never seen and you are not liking because she is weak and sickly?

WOW.

And then the photo came.

She sent him an AMAZING photo.

When I saw her I couldn't believe it. I saw that photo with my eyes. I swear on the Bible.

She was smiling with a baby by her side.

"And this baby? Didn't she have an only child?" I asked for.

"She actually has two children." He answered me. "He was afraid to show me the second one."

"Has he waited two years to teach you the child?"

"Yes."

"Damn Antonio ... That child is a baby. He is at most two months old. "

"Not. Is two years old."

"No Antonio. That's a baby. "

"You don't know about children. I have had 17 sons and daughters. I know about children and that's a two-year-old boy. "

WOW.

He really was more blind than Stevie Wonder.

Or was it a Superpendejo.

It was clear. The woman had a Sancho.

Antonio Toledo sent money and they ate seafood, parties, clothes, gifts and luxuries every two weeks: thousands of fresh dollars from the United States.

The whims that Antonio did not give because he lived as a miserable, they gave it to his health.

They fucked full of joy and she got pregnant. And she introduced him to her 2-year-old "Hidden Son" when in fact he was a two-month-old baby.

Surrealistic.

The most incredible thing is that Antonio defended before all his companions that this baby was a two-year-old boy.

Amazing.

And Antonio Toledo started another online relationship.

CHAPTER 13

2016
Dallas - Texas - United States

Antonio Toledo broke up with her because she was always sick and asking for money. That is what he told me.

I spoke as a friend to him: "Antonio... For ten years you have sent all your money to your ex-wife, about $ 170,000, then the woman from the farm appeared, another $ 200,000 in another ten years and now for two years about $ 35,000 to that black woman. who had a man behind. You have worked very hard in the United States and have lost more than $ 400,000 that you do not have. You should save for yourself. For your close withdrawal a money. Don't send more money to women. They are ripping you off and ruining you one after the other. "

He never heard me.

It was amazing because he never made a savings plan, a 401K or something like that.

In 23 years in the United States, he did not try to regularize his situation.

I'm not saying trying to be a citizen of the United States, but being a permanent resident.

At work we had a Mexican companion named Joel, who he told me never became a citizen but a resident, and counting on social security, in the end when he retired he would return to Mexico and receive a retirement check from the United States every month .

That was very thoughtful and smart. But Antonio Toledo never did any of it.

"Why?" I asked him.

His responses were:

A) Because I don't like the United States
B) Because I am not going to stay and live here
C) Because when I retire I will return to Nicaragua D) Because it is a stupid and unnecessary expense of money

I replied: "It doesn't matter if you don't like the United States or if you have no intention of living your old age here. All that is ok. But by spending a little money each month you ensure a retirement. That expense that you say is unnecessary when you return to Nicaragua, you are going to have a retirement check from the United States every month that will help you a lot."

And that logic did not understand or did not want to understand it.

The point is that it was too late: he would soon retire and not pay social security every month, he would not have any kind of pay in his old age.

Very sad.

A mindless strategy.

Other coworkers, Joel and García, rebuked him and told him. Palacios and Ortiz, both also Mexicans, also told him so.

But he didn't listen to anyone.

CHAPTER 14

2016

Dallas - Texas - United States

Then other girls appeared to him by texts on the phone, also from his town, and Antonio Toledo began another relationship.

He proudly showed his girlfriend photos.

They were photos of a twenty-year-old Hispanic girl, very fit, with clothes as if she were training fitness, with piercings and a tattoo.

She was a very beautiful and attractive woman, super fit, but they were obviously stolen photos from some Facebook profile.

One day talking, he commented that he did not like tattoos: that a woman with tattoos was the most disgusting thing in the world.

And I would say to him: "The girl in those photos has several, small, but several."

And he said NO.

That this girl did not have any tattoos and that I was blind and did not see well.

WOW.

He said that what he liked most about that girl is that she was a hard worker and from a good family, something very good, because when she retired and returned to Nicaragua, she was going to live comfortably and safely.

She sent several photos of her home, where she lived with her mother.

I saw those photos.

A house like that of the Kardashians in Pumpkins, California,

It had an amazing piano room.

In another photo there was a second room with different decoration.

A picture of marble-walled bathrooms with luxury German faucets was incredible. A millionaire house bathroom.

And in the photos I saw folds: taken directly with the camera of a phone to a magazine.

Others had watermarks. They were from decoration websites, houses and furniture.

I said to him: "Antonio... Those photos are not real. Those are photos taken from the Internet, from magazines. They are cheating on you. That is an online scam. "

And Antonio Toledo answered me: "What are you going to know about the Internet. What you have is envy. "

WOW.

Several times I tried to explain to her that the photos of the girl were from some internet or Facebook profile, of an athlete or professional model, and that the photos of the house were from some website and magazines.

There was no way. Very stubborn

He did not listen to reasons.

And he sent all his money to that supposed girl.

CHAPTER 15

2016
Dallas - Texas - United States

Then Antonio Toledo began to explain to everyone in his work the great business that his new wife did.

A wonderful woman because she was a hard worker, made a lot of money and knew how to manage businesses.

He boasted that she was exceptional and better than any other because she made a lot of money.

There were two businesses, he explained.

I bought bundles of used clothing from the United States. He sent the money, they sent a bundle of used clothes (nobody knew what garments were inside) and when the bundle of $ 100 arrived, he sold the garments individually. And it got a return of 300%. It cost $ 100, she took out $ 400, and she had $ 300 left clean. She sold four bales of clothing each month and made about $ 1,200 for her.

Where did you sell it?

Directly at his mansion.

He left the doors open, the townspeople entered, the peasants, and they bought the clothes in cash. He didn't have a store or was a showman He sold it directly to his home, according to her.

The second business was pouting food.

He would open the door to his mansion and people would come in, feed them, have a refrigerator with sodas and beers, feed them, and come loose tobacco cigarettes.

He would show them the pack of tobacco and they would take one, two or three cigarettes. Then he would charge them for food, drinks and cigarettes.

He made about $ 100 a day, about $ 3,000 a month.

I said to Antonio Toledo: "Wow ... Yes, she is a great businessman. $ 3,000 giving meals at home at noon and $ 1,200 in bales of used clothing, makes $ 4,200 a month. Many people do not earn that money in the United States every month. At Amazon, people working 40 hours a week, for $ 15 an hour less taxes, will make about $ 2,000 a month. That woman earns twice as much in Nicaragua as an Amazon worker in the United States! And considering that the standard of living is much lower and cheaper in Nicaragua, earning $ 4,200 in Nicaragua is like earning $ 10,000 a month in the United States. No wonder she has a large, beautiful, piano-like mansion there. ”

Antonio was laughing full of happiness and pride.

“Now do you understand? See the woman so excellent that I have found? A born business woman! ” He said proudly.

"And because if she makes so much money and lives in a mansion, do you have to send all your money to her every month?" Asked.

"You don't understand it. We are a couple, like a marriage. I have to send all my money there to show her that I trust her. She keeps everything, hers and mine, in the same bank account. ”

WOW.

CHAPTER 16

2016
Dallas - Texas - United States

One day working at the Hotel, some clients left things on a table, toys, Among them was an Aladdin-like golden plastic lamp.

Take the lamp and I showed it to Antonio Toledo: "Look, a lamp like Aladdin's. Do you know what to do with it? "

And he said: "Yes."

He looked at the long butt, put it in his mouth and started sucking on it. I shouted: "Antonio: that is not a feeding bottle. Disgusting ... What if someone has touched that? How do you put it in your mouth? "

He was laughing happily like a child sucking on the plastic lamp.

I remembered his anecdote years ago with the transvestite and came to the quick conclusion that something happened there!

One day Antonio Toledo told me anguished that the mobile phone did not work and was totally blocked. Not know what to do.

I offered to help him.

I thought he was so blind that he didn't know he would play on the phone and he had blocked it himself. Fixing that is not complicated at all.

And he gave me his phone. And I fixed it: He had indeed blocked it.

Readers will forgive me, but when faced with such an opportunity I could not resist. I know what I'm saying is unethical, but it was: I quickly looked at his phone.

What I saw was devastating.

Amazing.

Science fiction shit.

On WhatsApp he had dozens of accounts of girls and women talking to him.

They were very similar in content.

They showed photos from some Facebook profile, pornographic photos of women who did not have the same face or body, but he did not realize the difference of how blind he was.

The conversations were more or less like this:

"Hello Antonio. My name is Maria."

"Who gave you my number?"

"A friend. He told me that you are a very serious and compliant man. I am single: I need a man to take care of me. Are you serious ?"

"Yes of course. You don't have a husband? "

"Not. And so I am very hot. Are you hot, Antonio? I need a very hot male. I had so many needs."

"Of course I'm hot."

"Then you are already my husband. Don't talk to another one: you are mine. You love Me?"

"Yes I love you."

"Really? Don't lie to me and break my heart. "

"I really love you, Maria."

"Do you have another? I warn you that I am very jealous. My macho, my male is only mine. "

"No, I have no other. Only you."

"Very well: you are mine and I am your wife from now on. "

That's the way most of the conversations were.

He never asked which friend it was that had given him her number.

And like that, he had twenty more women on WhatsApp.

He sent everyone different amounts of money.

They talked about love and sent him pornographic photos, He sent dark photos in his room, lying on the bed, masturbating. He sent many photos of those to those women.

One of the Whatsapp accounts look inside the internal profile and the small round photo was of ... A man with a mustache!

WOW.

Those online scammers were no longer trying.

Those men knew that Antonio Toledo was so stupid and so blind, that they already created multi-accounts of women from their own profiles.

Very strong.

CHAPTER 17

2017
Dallas - Texas - United States

Antonio Toledo was 65 years old.

One day something terrible happened.

He called me on the phone crying: her 40-year-old son had been murdered in town. They had found him lying near a dirt soccer field, shot to death.

Do not go to Nicaragua.

He did not attend the funeral.

He couldn't pay even $ 20 from his own son's funeral. Because he sent all the money to Nicaragua to these women and lived daily, drinking tap water, listening to the same old radio and eating Maruchas.

That was very tragic.

I saw him cry and very sad. I felt sorry that this man will spend all his money he had earned in a lifetime for scammers on the Internet and could not even help in the burial of his own son.

Very strong.

My theory is that since he was from a small town, everyone knew everyone there.

Whether it was for the wife or for her 14 sons and daughters who would live there, they learned of the story that Antonio Toledo gave a mountain of money and in the end was never there, and he lost everything.

The second 35-year-old woman, the one from the farm and the donkey, got Antonio's phone number and tried her luck.

What you never thought was that you would win the casino's top prize: $ 200.00, house, land, and a farm.

Then he sent him for a walk and Antonio did not claim anything.

From there one can think many things.

A) Friends or relatives of the second woman contacted him.
B) That same woman created new identities and contacted him, to continue taking money from him.
C) The woman's Sancho created identities and contacted him. The female voice on the other side would be a family member or friend.
D) Town scammers, helped by friends, girlfriends, wives or relatives created identities and contacted him.

And that new woman, the fitness star, who owns a mansion and did incredible business, came up with something: she needed to expand her business.

The excuse: to generate more money for when Antonio Toledo definitively left for Nicaragua, he would have a beautiful mountain of money there to enjoy in his old age.

On the one hand, Antonio gave her money to buy bales: the merchant wanted to sell two bales a week and increase her income by $ 2,400 a month by selling used clothing.

I needed to sell more.

Friends of hers offered to sell clothes at their houses, so she needed a vehicle to move the bales of clothes throughout Nicaragua.

A Toyota Tacoma.

A 2012, five-year used, is worth depending on your state between $ 12,000 and $ 21,000.

The woman said it was only worth $ 5,000.

I said to him: "Antonio: if the 2012 Tacoma are worth $ 5,000 in Nicaragua, less than half that in the United States, I bought a dozen. I put them in a container and sell them in Dallas a little below the market price. I will win a lot of money. In Nicaragua they don't sell them: they give them away. "

He bought the Toyota Tacoma and received a photo taken on the street and by mail an invoice (I saw it with MY EYES) that was a page from a school pad, written in pen that said:

"THE TACOMA OF ANTONIO TOLEDO COST $ 5,000"

No signature, no stamp, no address, no Tacoma chassis number or license plate.

A few months later she told him that just in case a tire was punctured or the engine was damaged, the most logical thing to do was to buy another Tacoma.

And Antonio Toledo bought a second Tacoma for another $ 5,000.

When I saw the second photo it was the same as the first one.

But he said no: it was the same color but a more modern model.

Stubborn like an old mule.

His coworkers joked with him: "Antonio Toledo: businessman selling used clothing in Nicaragua, with his own fleet of Tacoma vehicles to distribute it."

He would be laughing at those jokes. He did not take them wrong.

CHAPTER 18

2017
Dallas - Texas - United States

Then something terrible happened to her at the age of 25:
she had a brain tumor that had to be operated on.

The operation cost a lot of money.

Mysteriously no one in her family had.

But she had all her savings. And he sold his majestic
palace. And with all this it was not enough for the
operation.

Antonio Toledo was going to fulfill as a serious man until
the last consequences. He could not allow his new wife,
the athlete, to die.

And left his apartment.

His moved into a tiny studio, and there he lived, without light. He did not pay electricity to save money. He lived in the dark and without air conditioning in summer in Dallas.

I asked him: "How can you live without air conditioning? It is hellishly hot. "

"I always have the windows open. The air that enters is very fresh. "

"And you are not afraid of being robbed?"

"Not."

I thought. "What are you going to steal? A shirt that is thirty years old? A radio older than Donald Duck's cap? A house the Maruchas? "

To save every last penny, Antonio Toledo lived without electricity or air conditioning. And he began to ask for money from all his colleagues to save the life of the athlete. Obviously Joel, Ortiz, etc... No one helped him.

Neither do I.

Then in front of everyone, she burst into desperate tears and screamed.

"SHE DYING! MY WOMAN IS DYING! "

That I was a witness and I saw it.

Ortiz, a Mexican coworker told me: "Antonio is sick. He has a mental illness."

A fellow from Puerto Rico, an asshole, left him $ 200.

And collecting money he sent $ 7,000 to Nicaragua for brain surgery.
I commented to him: "It is very cheap to have operations there. Here with $ 7,000 he doesn't even give you to pay the sandwich to the anesthetist. "

He stuck out his chest like a peacock: "In Nicaragua everything is cheaper."

After the operation, the athlete miraculously recovered: in a week like new.

It was terrifying.

Antonio Toledo lived without electricity, without light,
without air conditioning, drinking tap water, eating
Maruchas, borrowing money from everyone he knew and
sending everything along with his own to an online
scammer or scammer in Nicaragua

CHAPTER 19

2017

Dallas - Texas - United States

Of the previous online girlfriend he had, the black woman, said that he was now living with the mayor of the town.

With the mayor?

"No wonder: you've made her a millionaire." I said jokingly.

I spoke to him many times, seriously.

"Antonio ... You have been working in the United States for 25 years, very hard: you are an excellent worker. You have generated about $ 400,000 in all those years and you have not enjoyed it. You live like a poor man, like a beggar. You have never indulged or enjoyed yourself. You have never enjoyed that money. Everything has been for

women who have never taken advantage of you: they
have kept everything. ”

Now Antonio is 65 years old and what have you got?
NOTHING.

Not even at the time, many years ago, did you arrange
your retirement in the United States.

If you had done it even if you retired with nothing, at least
you would have a check from the United States, a good
amount of money in dollars, which in Nicaragua would be
a lot of money and would give you to live well.

“My recommendation is that you save for yourself, buy a
small apartment of $ 30,000 to live there when you are
old. And don't give anybody more money. ”

Do you know what he told me?

"Men don't have to have any money. The money must
have women. We men spend them on nonsense. Women
know very well how to manage money in a home. ”
Antonio said.

WOW.

I answered him: "Hell, Antonio. Men spend money on nonsense? You haven't bought yourself a shirt in decades. You, spending $ 10 on a McMenu, is unthinkable. You never spend money. What nonsense is it that you spend money on nonsense? "

He did not answer me.

"Antonio ... I make you a reflection and do not take it wrong." I told. "Imagine that in the end you retire, you go to Nicaragua, and that athlete disappears with all your money. You will have worked a lifetime in America for nothing. You will have no home, no money, no savings, no retirement check. How will you live there? "

He answered. "Well, I'm going to live with a relative of mine. No need to give me a room: I can sleep in the garage of the house, in the stables, in the barn or wherever. I am young and strong. I will return to work in the field and take out every day to eat. If I have a roof and food, it is enough for me. "

Terrible.

A life working in the United States, making a lot of money, to end up in old Nicaragua, sleeping with spiders in a smelly garage, and working in the fields for a plate of food.

And in that same year, 2017, I left that company in Dallas, to work in another in Fort Worth.

CHAPTER 20

2020
Dallas - Texas - United States

With the coronavirus COVID-19 pandemic, I called Antonio Toledo one day worrying about his health and how things are going for him.

He told me he was fine, he continued working in the same place with 68 years.

He was in good health and continued with the online girlfriend athlete.

Antonio Toledo never wanted to retire, he made that promise every year "Next year I retire" but he never did because he liked the money so much (but not spending it) that it was never enough for him.

And all the money was sent to that supposed woman who had never seen face to face, who had never hugged or kissed: four years with her.

Now, since she had sold her mansion for brain surgery, she had no home. Now he was no longer selling bales of used clothing, or meals with cigarettes at noon.

Companions of Antonio Toledo said to him: "Yes, in addition to feeding and eating cigarettes to the men who are going to eat at home, she also gives them all blowjobs, she can make even more money. Expand the business operations."

Antonio answered: "But how is she going to do that? She loves Me!"

Total that from 2017 to 2020 with all the money that Antonio Toledo had sent him, he had bought a not very large piece of land, built a three-bedroom house that connected next to a store with a metal shutter that went up and down.

At that store the fitness runner sold bulk beans, chickpeas, and lentils. He had sacks, filled paper bags, and weighed them.

Antonio was happy because he had a new house, not very big, unfortunately without a donkey, but with a small attached shop and two Tacomas to distribute vegetables throughout the town.

I imagined that the moment Antonio finally left for Nicaragua, the same would happen to him with the farmer. They would close the door on him and he would lose the house, the store and the savings in the bank.

EVERYTHING.

Again he would be left with nothing, because nothing was in his name.

In a realistic scenario, if Antonio saved a few thousand dollars on his part, when he got there to retire, Sancho and his friends would kidnap him and empty his bank card until he was penniless.

From there two things could happen: to let him go.

Antonio Toledo would look very old, without money and nothing in Nicaragua, totally ruined.

Or it could be that they killed him and since the town was in the mountains, with a lot of jungle and forest around it, they made a hole somewhere, they would bury it there and nobody would ever find it.

The question is ... Who would miss him?

His sons and daughters had no relationship with him, nor
did he have any relationship with his ex-wife.

No one would miss him.

AFTERWORD

That is the whole story of Antonio Toledo.

A 100% AUTHENTIC story.

What can we learn from it?

That on the Internet there are endless swindlers with multi-accounts that pretend to be women, the elderly, singles, etc... They invent incredible lies to ruthlessly steal money from ignorant, lonely and loveless people.

Superpendejos like Antonio Toledo.

Stupid people who steal their money over and over and never learn the lesson: very sad but I don't feel sorry for him, because he is an asshole, all his life and he will die being a great asshole.

Another lesson is that it is incredible that many people are desperate to live and work in the United States of America: they would do anything. It is their dream.

Antonio Toledo arrived legally and with a visa, and has earned a lot of money for nothing.

That's what I mean by a broken and wasted American dream.

A stupid man who instead of taking advantage of his life in the United States threw it down the sewer.

There is always the romantic and idealistic idea that from Mexico, Central and South America people come to work hard and earn a living to have a better future.

But assholes also come, with a great opportunity, and they don't take advantage of it.

Assholes like Antonio Toledo that all the money he earned with his hard work was for nothing, for scammers.

Very sad.

Imagine Antonio Toledo old, after working very hard a lifetime, with absolutely nothing. Pathetic.

I don't think a person like him deserves the opportunity to come to the United States.

A person who really takes it seriously deserves the opportunity.

An old man of more than 60 years with the fantasy that he wants a beautiful, hot and 20-year-old woman is a child's fantasy. A misogynist porn dream.

When he finally retired and back to Nicaragua: what kind of life can give a 70 years old man to a 25 years old athlete wife? What a fool!

I always told him: "Forget your porno fantasy. Instead of a 20 years old wife, find a 45 to 50 year old mature lady, a decade younger that you."

But he always answer me: "Why the hell I need a old woman?"

A man on his way to being blind because he is so unhappy, stingy, and miserable that he doesn't want to spend money on eye surgery.

A man who is a very good person and with a big heart and as I had a lot of appreciation for him and all his colleagues, for years we warned him.

We told him that all of these were online scammers. But he NEVER listened.

He turned a deaf ear to everything. The most stubborn and square head guy I have ever met in my life.

A Superpendejo.

Thank you very much for reading this book.

9 798711 705857